STATES

VIRGINIA

A MyReportLinks.com Book

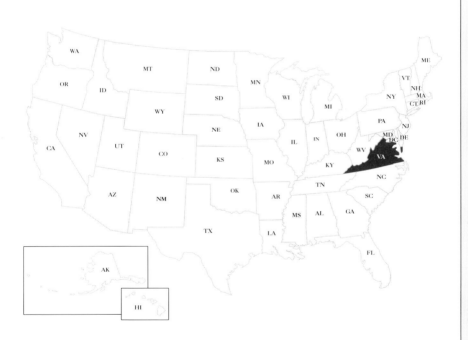

Kim A. O'Connell

MyReportLinks.com Books

an imprint of

Enslow Publishers, Inc.

Box 398, 40 Industrial Road
Berkeley Heights, NJ 07922
USA

MyReportLinks.com Books, an imprint of Enslow Publishers, Inc. MyReportLinks is a trademark of Enslow Publishers, Inc.

Library of Congress Cataloging-in-Publication Data

O'Connell, Kim A.
    Virginia / Kim A. O'Connell.
        p. cm. — (States)
Includes bibliographical references and index.
Contents: Virginia : witness to history —Mountains to the sea : Virginia's land and climate —Tobacco to technology : Virginia's economy — For the good of the commonwealth : Virginia's government — Liberty or death : Virginia history.
    ISBN 0-7660-5122-6
    1. Virginia—Juvenile literature. [1. Virginia.] I. Title. II. States (Series : Berkeley Heights, N.J.)
    F226.3 .O27 2003
    975.5—dc21
                        2002007478

Printed in the United States of America

10 9 8 7 6 5 4 3 2 1

To Our Readers:
Through the purchase of this book, you and your library gain access to the Report Links that specifically back up this book.

The Publisher will provide access to the Report Links that back up this book and will keep these Report Links up to date on **www.myreportlinks.com** for three years from the book's first publication date.

We have done our best to make sure all Internet addresses in this book were active and appropriate when we went to press. However, the author and the Publisher have no control over, and assume no liability for, the material available on those Internet sites or on other Web sites they may link to.

The usage of the MyReportLinks.com Books Web site is subject to the terms and conditions stated on the Usage Policy Statement on **www.myreportlinks.com**.

In the future, a password may be required to access the Report Links that back up this book. The password is found on the bottom of page 4 of this book.

Any comments or suggestions can be sent by e-mail to comments@myreportlinks.com or to the address on the back cover.

Photo Credits: © 2001 Robesus, Inc., p. 10 (flag); © Corel Corporation, p. 3; Dover Publications, Inc., p. 40; Enslow Publishers, Inc., pp. 1 (map), 17; Gunston Hall Plantation, p. 36; Library of Congress, pp. 20, 31, 34; MyReportLinks.com Books, p. 4; Robert E. Lee Memorial Association, p. 13; U.S. Department of Defense, p. 44; Virginia Historical Society, pp. 11, 14, 38; Virginia Tourism Corporation, pp. 16, 18, 22, 24, 25, 27, 37; Virtual Jamestown, p. 29; White House Historical Association, p. 31.

Cover Photo: Colonial Williamsburg Foundation

Cover Description: The Governor's Palace, Williamsburg

Contents

MyReportLinks.com Books
Great Books, Great Links, Great for Research!

MyReportLinks.com Books present the information you need to learn about your report subject. In addition, they show you where to go on the Internet for more information. The pre-evaluated Report Links that back up this book are kept up to date on **www.myreportlinks.com**. With the purchase of a MyReportLinks.com Books title, you and your library gain access to the Report Links that specifically back up that book. The Report Links save hours of research time and link to dozens—even hundreds—of Web sites, source documents, and photos related to your report topic.

Please see "To Our Readers" on the Copyright page for important information about this book, the MyReportLinks.com Books Web site, and the Report Links that back up this book.

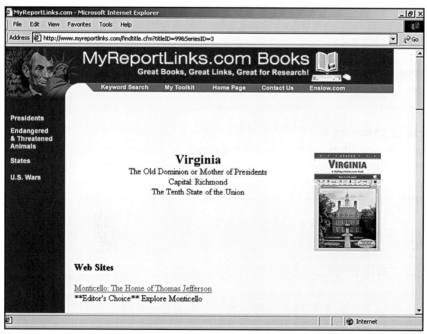

Access:

The Publisher will provide access to the Report Links that back up this book and will try to keep these Report Links up to date on our Web site for three years from the book's first publication date. Please enter **SVA3957** if asked for a password.

Report Links

The Internet sites described below can be accessed at
http://www.myreportlinks.com

*EDITOR'S CHOICE

▶ Monticello: The Home of Thomas Jefferson
At this Web site you can explore the history of Monticello, Thomas
Jefferson's magnificent home in Charlottesville, Virginia, considered
one of the finest examples of neoclassical architecture.

Link to this Internet site from http://www.myreportlinks.com

*EDITOR'S CHOICE

▶ Explore the State: Virginia
America's Story from America's Library, a Library of Congress Web site,
offers interesting anecdotes about Virginia's history.

Link to this Internet site from http://www.myreportlinks.com

*EDITOR'S CHOICE

▶ Stratford Hall—The Birthplace of Robert E. Lee
Stratford Hall Plantation, in southeastern Virginia, is the ancestral
home of the Lee Family and the birthplace of Robert E. Lee. This site
offers a tour of the plantation, a history of the Lees of Virginia, and
provides links to other historical resources.

Link to this Internet site from http://www.myreportlinks.com

*EDITOR'S CHOICE

▶ Virtual Jamestown
This Web site offers a virtual journey through Jamestown, Virginia, as
it was in the seventeenth century. Included are many primary source
materials, including maps, images, court records, labor contracts, public
records, first-hand accounts of settlers, and letters.

Link to this Internet site from http://www.myreportlinks.com

*EDITOR'S CHOICE

▶ Virginia Historical Society
The Virginia Historical Society Web site presents online changing
exhibitions that capture Virginia's history in documents, photographs,
and letters.

Link to this Internet site from http://www.myreportlinks.com

*EDITOR'S CHOICE

▶ Colonial Williamsburg History
Colonial Williamsburg is a living-history museum that re-creates life in
eighteenth-century Williamsburg, the original capital of Virginia.
Colonial Williamsburg's Web site offers information about the museum
itself and contains historical documents about colonial life in America.

Link to this Internet site from http://www.myreportlinks.com

Report Links

▶ **Arlington National Cemetery**

At the Arlington National Cemetery Web site you will find information about the cemetery, the resting place for many of America's war heroes, as well as a list of persons buried there.

Link to this Internet site from http://www.myreportlinks.com

▶ **Civil War Traveler in Virginia**

At this Web site you can learn about the Civil War battles fought in many areas of Virginia. Maps and information about key participants are included.

Link to this Internet site from http://www.myreportlinks.com

▶ **Death at Jamestown**

This PBS Web site offers a brief history of Jamestown. Here you will learn about the challenges that the colonists faced and find images of the fort as it might have looked. You can also take an interactive tour of Jamestown.

Link to this Internet site from http://www.myreportlinks.com

▶ **Flowerdew Hundred**

Flowerdew Hundred was one of the first Virginia land grants. This virtual museum interprets the area's history through stories and a collection of artifacts.

Link to this Internet site from http://www.myreportlinks.com

▶ **Fredericksburg and Spotsylvania National Military Park**

This National Park Service Web site provides detailed information about the Fredericksburg and Spotsylvania National Military Park. Here you can explore the history of the park as well as the Civil War battles fought there.

Link to this Internet site from http://www.myreportlinks.com

▶ **The Geography of Virginia's Slave Market**

At this Web site you can explore Virginia's slave trade during the nineteenth century through a series of tables, graphs, and maps.

Link to this Internet site from http://www.myreportlinks.com

Report Links

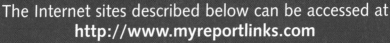

The Internet sites described below can be accessed at
http://www.myreportlinks.com

▶ **The Geology of Virginia**
Explore Virginia's geology through photographs, maps, and diagrams.
Also included are articles and narratives.

Link to this Internet site from http://www.myreportlinks.com

▶ **Gunston Hall—The Home of George Mason**
Tour Gunston Hall Plantation, in Mason Neck, Virginia, the home of
George Mason. Mason's ideas on human rights, as seen in his draft of the
Virginia Declaration of Rights, written in 1776, did much to influence the
thinking of the founding fathers, including Thomas Jefferson.

Link to this Internet site from http://www.myreportlinks.com

▶ **Jamestown Historic Briefs**
This National Park Service Web site provides an in-depth history of
Jamestown. Here you will find time lines and profiles of Jamestown
settlers and learn about the historical significance of Jamestown.

Link to this Internet site from http://www.myreportlinks.com

▶ **Jamestown Rediscovery**
At this Web site you can explore the history of Jamestown, learn about
archaeological findings there, view exhibits, and much more.

Link to this Internet site from http://www.myreportlinks.com

▶ **Kids Cave**
Kids Cave offers information for kids in Virginia about ways to
prevent pollution and offers facts about recycling, rivers, and waste
management in the commonwealth.

Link to this Internet site from http://www.myreportlinks.com

▶ **Manassas**
This Web site takes viewers to the Manassas National Battlefield Park.
The park has preserved the sites of two major Civil War battles fought
in the Manassas, Virginia, countryside. You will also find descriptions
of the battles and a list of casualties by brigade or division.

Link to this Internet site from http://www.myreportlinks.com

Report Links

▶ **Meet Amazing Americans: Pocahontas**
America's Story from America's Library, a Library of Congress Web site, tells the story of Pocahontas, daughter of Chief Powhatan, who promoted peace between the Powhatan Indians and the English colonists at Jamestown.

Link to this Internet site from http://www.myreportlinks.com

▶ **My Virginia**
The official Commonwealth of Virginia home page provides access to all of Virginia's government services, including information about businesses, family services, and education.

Link to this Internet site from http://www.myreportlinks.com

▶ **The Pentagon**
The Pentagon in Arlington, Virginia, is the headquarters of the United States Department of Defense—the home of America's military leaders. The Pentagon's official Web site includes facts and figures, photographs, and a virtual tour of the facility, one of the largest office complexes in the world.

Link to this Internet site from http://www.myreportlinks.com

▶ **Robert Edward Lee: Biography**
Robert Edward Lee, born in Stratford, Virginia, is generally considered one of the greatest figures of the Civil War. Lee's ancestors played an important role in Virginia's and America's history. This site provides a brief biography of Lee along with links to additional information about him.

Link to this Internet site from http://www.myreportlinks.com

▶ **Shenandoah National Park**
Shenandoah National Park is located in Virginia's Blue Ridge Mountains. This National Park Service Web site gives the park's history, describes local flora and fauna, and includes other relevant information.

Link to this Internet site from http://www.myreportlinks.com

▶ **Stately Knowledge: Virginia**
This Web site provides basic facts about Virginia. You will also find an image of the state flag and links to additional Internet resources.

Link to this Internet site from http://www.myreportlinks.com

Report Links

The Internet sites described below can be accessed at
http://www.myreportlinks.com

▶ **Tribes of Virginia**
Virginia has eight recognized American Indian tribes. This page
provides access to the official sites of each of the eight tribes: the
Chickahominy, Eastern Chickahominy, Mattaponi, Monacan,
Nansemond, Pamunkey, Rappahanock, and Upper Mattaponi.

Link to this Internet site from http://www.myreportlinks.com

▶ **U.S. Census Bureau: Virginia**
The United States Census Bureau provides statistics on Virginia's
people, economy, and geography.

Link to this Internet site from http://www.myreportlinks.com

▶ **Virginia Places**
This site presents a captivating and in-depth analysis of Virginia's
demographics and population patterns since 1790. Statistics, tables,
and additional links on the subject are included.

Link to this Internet site from http://www.myreportlinks.com

▶ **Virginia State Parks**
Virginia is home to forty-four state parks and recreation areas, enjoyed
by residents of and visitors to the commonwealth. This Web site serves
as an interactive guide to the state's park system.

Link to this Internet site from http://www.myreportlinks.com

▶ **Virginia: Tidal Wetlands Impact Data**
Wetlands management is a national challenge. This site provides
information about the tidal wetlands of Virginia, home to many plant
and animal species, and tells what is being done to manage and
conserve them.

Link to this Internet site from http://www.myreportlinks.com

▶ **Yorktown Is Won!**
This Web site offers an account of the British surrender at Yorktown,
Virginia, which marked the end of the fighting in the Revolutionary War.

Link to this Internet site from http://www.myreportlinks.com

Virginia Facts

Capital
Richmond

Population
7,078,515*

Beverage
Milk

Bird
Northern cardinal

Dog
American foxhound

Fish
Brook trout

Flower and Tree
American dogwood

Insect
Tiger swallowtail butterfly

Motto
Sic Semper Tyrannis
("Thus Always to Tyrants")

Nicknames
Old Dominion; Mother of
Presidents; Mother of States

Shell
Oyster

Song
Virginia currently has no state
song. "Carry Me Back to Old
Virginia," adopted as the state
song in 1940, was retired by
the Virginia General Assembly
in 1997 because of lyrics about
slavery that many Virginians
found offensive.

Flag
The flag features the Virginia
state seal, in which the Roman
goddess Virtus, dressed as an
Amazon, stands over the fallen
body of Tyranny, on a blue
background with the state
motto, adopted in 1931.

*Population reflects the 2000 census.

Tools

Search
Notes

Discuss
MyReportLinks.com Books
Go!

Chapter 1 ▶

Virginia: Witness to History

Few states combine natural beauty and historical importance the way Virginia does. Located in the Mid-Atlantic region of the United States, Virginia is made up of rugged mountains, rolling farmland, marshy swamps, and sandy coastlines. But the state also has sites related to some

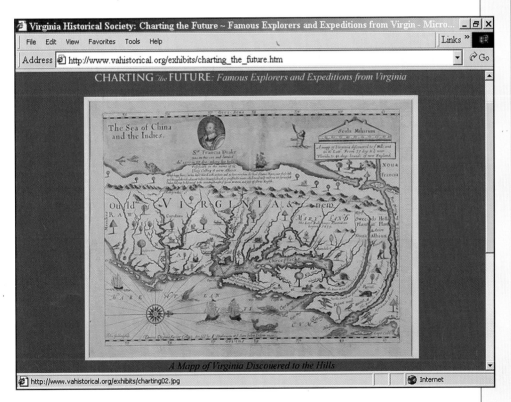

▲ This 1651 map of Virginia shows Virginia close to the Pacific Ocean. At the time, some mapmakers thought America was just a short land bridge away from Asia.

of our nation's most important political and military events. The first permanent English settlement in America was built along the shores of the James River, one of Virginia's most important waterways. The state's American Indian history includes such legendary figures as Pocahontas and Powhatan. Key battles of the American Revolution and the Civil War took place here. And Virginians either wrote or helped to develop the Declaration of Independence and the U.S. Constitution.

Like its first colonists, the state's name has its roots in England. When Sir Walter Raleigh, England's famed adventurer, first landed on American shores in 1584, he dubbed the land "Virginia," in honor of Queen Elizabeth I, who had never married and was known as the Virgin Queen. Virginia was the first of the thirteen original colonies. Over time, the large Virginia colony was divided into other states, including Illinois, Indiana, Kentucky, Michigan, Minnesota, Ohio, West Virginia, and Wisconsin. For this, Virginia is often called "the mother of states," although its most common nickname is "Old Dominion." According to the state constitution, Virginia is a commonwealth, a designation also held by three other states—Kentucky, Massachusetts, and Pennsylvania.

▶ The Mother of Presidents

Virginia, known as the mother of states, is also the "mother of presidents." Eight presidents of the United States were born in Virginia. George Washington, the nation's first president, was born in Westmoreland County. Thomas Jefferson, the author of the Declaration of Independence and the third president, was born in what is today Albemarle County. James Madison, the fourth president, and James Monroe, the fifth, were from King

George and Westmoreland Counties, respectively. William Henry Harrison, the ninth president, who died a month after he 'was inaugurated, and his successor, John Tyler, were both from Charles City County. Zachary Taylor, the twelfth president and Mexican-American War hero, was from Orange County. Finally, Woodrow Wilson, the twenty-eighth president, who guided the nation through World War I, was born in Staunton, Virginia.

▶ Other Famous Virginians

Many other Virginians have contributed to the nation's political and military history. In 1775, Patrick Henry, a

History of Stratford Hall Plantation and the Lees of Virginia - Microsoft Internet Explorer

File   Edit   View   Favorites   Tools   Help   Links »

Address http://www.stratfordhall.org/history.htm   Go

Stratford
and the Lees of Virginia
a brief history

Thomas Lee (1690-1750) was a founder of the Ohio Company, a member of the governing Council of the colony, and acting Governor of Virginia. In 1717, he purchased the land for Stratford Hall Plantation and, during the period of 1730-1738, built the brick Georgian Great House. At the Stratford Landing on the Potomac River, he built a wharf and grist mill. A successful tobacco planter and land speculator, he owned more than 16,000 acres in Virginia and Maryland. The labor force was made up of slaves, indentured servants, and transported convicts.

Thomas Lee and his wife, Hannah, raised a remarkable family of six sons and two daughters. Their eldest son, Philip Ludwell Lee (1727-1775), inherited Stratford. Richard Henry and Francis Lightfoot Lee were the only brothers to sign the Declaration of Independence. Thomas Ludwell Lee helped write Virginia's resolves for independence and was one of the first judges elected to Virginia's supreme court. William and Arthur Lee were both diplomats working to secure the European support during the Revolution. Hannah Lee Corbin was a proponent of women's rights. Her sister, Alice Lee, married Dr. William Shippen of Philadelphia, who served as chief physician and director general of the Continental Army hospitals.

Philip Ludwell Lee was a planter and member of the Council of Virginia. A lover of horses, he imported the English race horse, Dotterel, and expanded the stables. He also continued

Thomas Lee

to develop the Landing.

Soon after the death of Philip Ludwell Lee, Stratford Hall Plantation became the home of his eldest daughter, the "divine Matilda" who married her cousin, Revolutionary War hero, "Light Horse Harry" Lee. She died in 1790, leaving her husband a life interest in the Plantation. In 1793, "Light Horse Harry"

 s ownership!   Internet

▲ *Stratford Hall Plantation is the ancestral home of the Lee family. In 1807, it was the birthplace of Robert E. Lee, the commanding general of the Confederate forces in the Civil War.*

lawyer and patriot, urged Virginians to fight for their independence with the famous phrase "Give me liberty or give me death!" In 1831, Nat Turner, a slave and preacher, led a bloody rebellion that helped widen the divide between those who supported slavery and those who opposed it. During the Civil War, many Virginians became famous as leaders of the Confederacy, including Robert E. Lee, Thomas "Stonewall" Jackson, and George Pickett. In the twentieth century, Harry F. Byrd, Sr., served in the U.S. Senate for more than thirty years. In 1989, L. Douglas Wilder became the first African American elected governor in the United States.

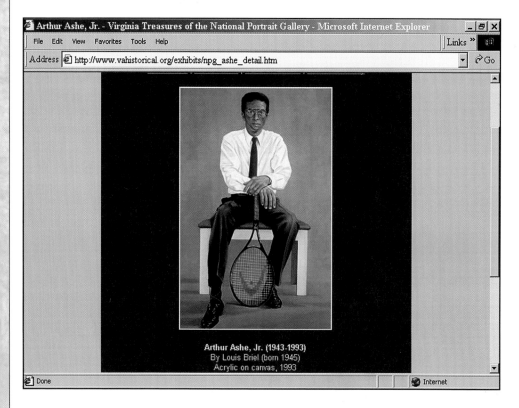

Arthur Ashe, Jr. - Virginia Treasures of the National Portrait Gallery - Microsoft Internet Explorer

File   Edit   View   Favorites   Tools   Help   Links »

Address http://www.vahistorical.org/exhibits/npg_ashe_detail.htm   Go

Arthur Ashe, Jr. (1943-1993)
By Louis Briel (born 1945)
Acrylic on canvas, 1993

Done   Internet

Tennis great Arthur Ashe was born in Richmond, Virginia.

Tools   Search   Notes   Discuss   Go!

But Virginians have also gained fame in other fields. Virginia has served as the birthplace or homeland of tennis player Arthur Ashe and basketball star Moses Malone; broadcaster Katie Couric; actors Shirley MacLaine and Warren Beatty; writer Willa Cather; singers Roy Clark, Ella Fitzgerald, and Patsy Cline; and dancer Bill "Bojangles" Robinson, among others.

Important Places

Virginia has protected and restored many sites related to the important people and events of its history. Tourists who visit Colonial Williamsburg, with its reconstructed homes and shops, can witness a re-creation of colonial life. Williamsburg, in the southeastern part of Virginia, served as the state capital from 1699 to 1780. Nearby is the Yorktown battlefield, the site of the final battle of the Revolutionary War and the surrender of the British army. Further north near Washington, D.C., George Washington's home, Mount Vernon, is open to tours of both the stately house and its elegant grounds. Arlington National Cemetery, just across the Potomac River from the nation's capital, contains the gravesites of many famous Americans, including President John F. Kennedy.

Countryside and Seaside

Virginia's hilly countryside includes many tourist attractions as well. Near Charlottesville, visitors can tour Thomas Jefferson's home and plantation, Monticello, considered one of the finest examples of American architecture. Civil War battlefields can be found near Manassas and Richmond in the eastern half of the state and up and down the Shenandoah Valley in the west. Along the ridge of the Blue Ridge Mountains, visitors can travel along

▲ *Perched atop a hill overlooking the Potomac River stands Mount Vernon, the home of George and Martha Washington.*

scenic Skyline Drive and the Blue Ridge Parkway. Natural Bridge is a 215-foot-tall natural stone arch in the southwestern part of the state. Along the coast, the Chesapeake Bay and the Atlantic Ocean offer plenty of opportunities for swimming, boating, fishing, and crabbing.

Virginia, steeped in history and rich in natural beauty, continues to thrive as a center of technology, government, tourism, and agriculture. "The good old dominion," Thomas Jefferson once wrote of his home state, "the blessed mother of us all."[1]

Chapter 2 ▶

Mountains to the Sea: Land and Climate

Virginia, one of the largest states on the East Coast, is shaped like a long triangle. From the Appalachian Mountains in the west to the Coastal Plain in the east, Virginia is 39,598 square miles. Virginia's highest point is Mount Rogers in the southwestern part of the state. At 5,729 feet, it towers over nearby towns. The state's lowest point is sea level along the coast. Virginia is bordered by West Virginia and Kentucky to the west; Washington, D.C., and Maryland to the east; and Tennessee and North Carolina to the south.

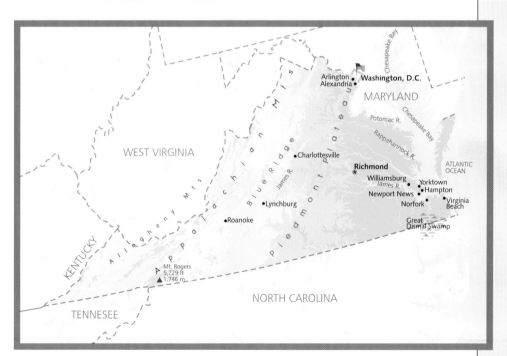

▲ A map of Virginia.

Mountains and Hills

Nearly parallel lines of mountain ranges form the western part of Virginia. These ranges are just a portion of the Appalachian Mountains, which stretch from Maine to Georgia. The Appalachians were once tall and rugged like the Rocky Mountains in the West, but over millions of years they have eroded into the rounded ridges seen in Virginia today. Moving west, the first mountain range is the Blue Ridge, followed by the Allegheny Mountains, which straddle the border with West Virginia.

In 1935 the federal government protected the landscape of the Blue Ridge by creating Shenandoah National Park. The name "Shenandoah" comes from an American

▲ At 5,729 feet, Mount Rogers, in the southwestern Blue Ridge Mountains, is the highest point in Virginia. The mountain is named for William Barton Rogers, Virginia's first state geologist.

Indian word that means "daughter of the stars." Skyline Drive is a 105-mile road that winds along the crest of the park and joins the Blue Ridge Parkway at the park's south end, which takes travelers southward into the mountains of North Carolina. In the spring, visitors to Shenandoah National Park can see the park blossom with purple rhododendron and flowering dogwood (the state tree). In the fall, the mountainsides come alive with flaming red and yellow leaves.

The valleys between these mountain ranges are just as interesting as the mountains themselves. The largest of these is the Shenandoah Valley, which contains fertile farmlands that lie along the Shenandoah River. The Shenandoah Valley also has its secrets: Hidden along the ridges and mountain gaps are miles of twisting underground caverns, including Luray Caverns, known for amazing natural colors and ten-foot-high ceilings.

To the east of the mountains is Virginia's Piedmont region. The name "Piedmont," from the French for "foot of the mountain," is a good characterization of the gently rising landscape that leads to the Blue Ridge Mountains. Richmond, the state capital, and Charlottesville are found in this region.

▶ Down by the Shore

In 1607, when a group of English colonists first saw the mouth of the James River and the Chesapeake Bay stretching before them, they were impressed by the area's natural beauty. George Percy, an investor in the Virginia colony, wrote about the land's "faire meaddowes and goodly tall Trees, with such Fresh-waters running through the woods."[1] These lowlands are referred to as the Tidewater region, because ocean water is pushed into the rivers with

the tides. Several of the state's longest and most important rivers—including the Potomac, the Rappahannock, the York, and the James—divide Tidewater Virginia into several peninsulas that jut into the Chesapeake Bay.

The Chesapeake Bay is a resource that is shared by Virginia and Maryland. At 193 miles long and up to 25 miles wide, Chesapeake Bay is the largest estuary in the nation. On the eastern side of the bay is Virginia's Eastern Shore, the southern part of the Delmarva Peninsula, so-named because Delaware, Maryland, and Virginia share it. This peninsula is lined with barrier islands. One of these islands, Chincoteague, was made famous in Marguerite

Wild ponies running along the shore of the Chincoteague National Wildlife Refuge on Assateague Island.

Henry's book *Misty of Chincoteague,* about an annual event in which wild ponies that live on nearby Assateague Island are rounded up, swum across a channel, and sold at auction.

South of Norfolk lies a part of Virginia that sounds as if it belongs in a fairy tale: the Great Dismal Swamp. The swamp is one of the best places in Virginia to see native animal species, including otters, bats, white-tailed deer, and black bears. The poisonous cottonmouth and copper-head snakes can be found here, too, as well as dozens of species of turtles, lizards, frogs, and toads.

▶ The Four Seasons

Virginia is almost ideally situated as a place to experience four complete seasons. Few states can claim such a diverse climate, with high temperatures and humidity, characteristic of the South, and cold, icy winters like those of the North. In between, however, are pleasantly mild springs and falls. Average temperatures, which vary from the mountains to the Tidewater, range from 70°F to 80°F in the summer and are around 36°F in the winter. The hottest temperature on record is 110°F at Balcony Falls in July 1954. The coldest was –30°F at Mountain Lake in January 1985.

Average annual precipitation in Virginia is 43 inches. In winter, it snows regularly only in the mountains, but every other part of Virginia has weathered a heavy blizzard every few years or so.

▶ Protecting the Environment

Although Virginia is still a beautiful state, its scenic landscapes are suffering from many environmental threats. As the state's population continues to rise, smog, sprawling development, and water pollution increase as well. In

▲ *The Great Dismal Swamp, in southern Virginia and northern North Carolina, has long been the subject of lore and legend.*

recent decades, acid rain has killed sensitive aquatic wildlife in Shenandoah National Park. Urban development has crowded and polluted Civil War battlefields at Manassas and around Richmond. Chemical runoff from farms and cities has polluted the waters of the Chesapeake Bay.

The state government, along with citizens and community groups, is working to protect these sites. In 1992, for example, the state introduced a popular license plate that features a crab, oysters, and sea grass with the words "Friend of the Chesapeake." A portion of the money collected from the sale of each license plate goes to the Chesapeake Bay Restoration Fund.

Chapter 3 ▶

Tobacco to Technology: Economy

For most of Virginia's history, the state's economy has centered on one crop and one crop alone: tobacco. American Indians were already growing tobacco in the Virginia region by the time English colonists landed at Jamestown, in 1607, and the colony soon picked up the practice. By the twentieth century, however, more and more jobs could be found in government and manufacturing. As the century ended, northern Virginia had become a hub of technology as well.

▶ Down on the Farm

Although Sir Walter Raleigh's first Virginia settlement on Roanoke Island did not last, it was successful in at least one way—Raleigh brought tobacco back to England. Although King James I later said tobacco smoke was "loathsome to the eye, hateful to the nose, harmful to the brain . . . [and] dangerous to the lungs," Queen Elizabeth I marveled that the plant was a "vegetable of singular strength and power."[1] Over the years, many farmers have felt the same way as the queen, because tobacco remains one of Virginia's most important crops. Grown primarily in the southern Piedmont region, tobacco produces more income for the state's farms than any other crop. Cigarette factories in Richmond contribute greatly to Virginia's tobacco industry as well.

Virginia has about 48,000 farms, covering about a third of the state's land area. In addition to tobacco, crops including corn, hay, peanuts, and soybeans are grown

▲ *More than half the apple orchards in Virginia are in the Shenandoah Valley, pictured above.*

on fields throughout Virginia. But the state has also developed regionalized crops. For example, more than half the apple orchards in the state are located in the Shenandoah Valley. Potatoes and tomatoes are grown near the Chesapeake Bay.

Most of Virginia's farm income comes from livestock and livestock products, however. The state is known for its production of young chickens, known as broilers, which are raised primarily in Rockingham County. Beef cattle are farmed in the western part of the state, and hogs are raised mostly in eastern Virginia. Land that is not taken up by farming may be put to use for mining. Coal and crushed stone are the most commonly mined products in the state.

As important as the land is to Virginia's economy, the state owes much to its waterways as well. Hampton Roads is Virginia's leading fishing port, bringing in crabs, oysters, striped bass, clams, and scallops, in addition to other fish and shellfish. Each year, fishing contributes more than $100 million to the state's economy.

▶ Keeping Things Going

Although headquartered in Washington, D.C., the federal government has a large presence in northern Virginia. The Pentagon, workplace to about 23,000 employees, is located in Arlington, and the Central Intelligence Agency is located in nearby McLean. Military bases include the Norfolk Naval Base and the Marine Corps base at Quantico.

Transportation also provides many jobs in Virginia. Two of the nation's largest railroad companies are based in Virginia, CSX in Richmond and Norfolk Southern in Norfolk. Virginia Railway Express, headquartered

▲ Fishing contributes more than $100 million annually to Virginia's economy. This photograph was taken in the waters off Hampton Roads, Virginia's leading port.

in Alexandria, is a commuter train that transports people from Manassas and Fredericksburg to and from Washington, D.C.

Virginia's 55,000 miles of roads and highways include the Little River Turnpike, the nation's first toll road, and the Chesapeake Bay Bridge-Tunnel, an 18-mile connector between the Eastern Shore and Norfolk.

In addition to major airports in Norfolk and Richmond, northern Virginia claims two of the busiest airports in the nation—Ronald Reagan Washington National Airport in Arlington and Washington Dulles International Airport in Herndon. U.S. Airways, one of the largest carriers in the country, is based in Arlington. Norfolk, Newport News, Hampton Roads, Alexandria, and Richmond are important ports for ships and boats large and small.

▶ Other Important Industries

The state's unofficial motto is "Virginia Is for Lovers," and this is especially true of people who love history and nature. Tourism is a growing part of Virginia's economy. Visitors come to Virginia to tour Civil War battlefields, Shenandoah National Park and the Blue Ridge Parkway, Colonial Williamsburg, and the Atlantic beaches. In just one recent year, for example, more than 1.5 million people visited Shenandoah, and more than 830,000 people visited the Manassas National Battlefield, the site of two major Civil War battles. Virginia also has thirty-four state parks and thirty-three natural areas, visited by more than 6.3 million people in 2000.

Communication is also a vital part of Virginia's economy. Several major newspapers are published in the state, including the *Richmond Times-Dispatch* and

▲ The Chesapeake Bay Bridge-Tunnel carries travelers from Virginia's Eastern Shore to the Virginia Beach-Norfolk area. More than seventeen miles long from shore to shore, it was heralded as an engineering wonder when it was completed in 1964. A parallel bridge-tunnel crossing was opened in 1999.

the *Virginian-Pilot*. The only national newspaper in the United States, *USA Today*, is headquartered in McLean. The state is also home to approximately 260 radio stations, 55 television stations, and 165 cable stations.

▶ A Technology Hub

Technology will become an increasingly important aspect of Virginia's economy. Already, northern Virginia is home to several major technology companies, including Internet giant America Online (AOL). When AOL expanded its facility in Prince William County in 1999, the state's technology secretary said that the expansion "further cements Virginia's role as the Internet Capital of the World."[2]

Chapter 4 ▶ The Good of the Commonwealth: Government

Virginia's state legislature, known as the General Assembly, is the oldest representative legislature in the United States. A representative legislature, in which people vote for those who are going to represent them in government, is the foundation of our nation's democracy. Virginia's General Assembly was formed when the colony was still ruled by England.

The years between 1614 and 1620 were prosperous ones for the young Virginia colony. The settlement at Jamestown, supported by a group of British investors called the Virginia Company of London, grew rapidly. Tobacco was exported to England, and plantations began to thrive along the James River. By 1618, the colony had grown so much that the Virginia Company of London allowed the creation of a governing body made up of representatives elected by the colonists. The House of Burgesses, as the governing body was called, met for the first time in July 1619. Although it could not enact laws that conflicted with those of England, the legislature was given the power to "make and ordaine whatsoever lawes and orders should . . . be thought good and proffittable for our subsistence."[1]

▶ The Legislative Branch

The modern Virginia General Assembly consists of two houses, the Senate and the House of Delegates. The Senate has 40 members who serve four-year terms, and the House of Delegates has 100 members who serve two-year terms.

Tools   Search   Notes   Discuss   Go!

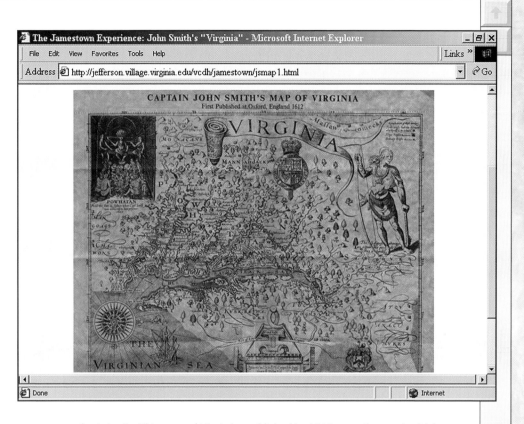

The Jamestown Experience: John Smith's "Virginia" - Microsoft Internet Explorer

File   Edit   View   Favorites   Tools   Help   Links »

Address http://jefferson.village.virginia.edu/vcdh/jamestown/jsmap1.html   Go

CAPTAIN JOHN SMITH'S MAP OF VIRGINIA
First Published at Oxford, England 1612

Done   Internet

John Smith's map of Virginia, published in 1612, was the most widely circulated map of Virginia for much of the seventeenth century. Many of Smith's place names are still used today.

The assembly makes all state laws, approves the state budget and decides how it is spent through a process called appropriations, and approves changes to the state constitution.

In fact, Virginia has updated its constitution regularly. The first state constitution was ratified in 1776, with other versions established in 1830, 1851, 1869, and 1902. The most recent version of the state constitution was ratified in 1970. The current constitution calls for environmental protection and annual legislative sessions. It also enforces the state's compliance with the national

Voting Rights Act of 1965, which lifted barriers that made it difficult for African Americans to vote.

On a national level, the state's representatives in Congress are two senators and eleven representatives.

▶ The Executive Branch

Until 1851, the General Assembly was also responsible for choosing the state governor. Since then, the state's governors—as well as lieutenant governors and attorneys general—have been elected by popular vote. Governors are elected to a four-year term and may not serve two terms in a row.

Some of the most significant people in American history have served as governor of Virginia, including U.S. presidents Thomas Jefferson, James Monroe, and John Tyler. More recent governors include Charles Robb, who increased spending on education and environmental protection; Gerald Baliles, who appointed the first woman to the Virginia Supreme Court; Douglas Wilder, the first African-American governor in U.S. history; George Allen, who pushed for economic growth; and Jim Gilmore, who worked to cut taxes.

The only person in Virginia history to serve two terms as governor was Mills E. Godwin, Jr., who also changed political parties. In his first term, from 1966 to 1970, he was a Democrat, but by his second term, 1974 to 1978, Godwin had become a Republican. Godwin's shift in parties is representative of the general political shift that has taken place in Virginia. For most of Virginia's history, the Democratic Party has dominated state politics. The state had only five Republican governors in the twentieth century, all in recent decades. The Republican Party continues to gain prominence in state politics.

Despite this trend, in 2002, Virginians welcomed Mark R. Warner, a Democrat, into the governor's mansion. As Virginia's sixty-ninth governor, Warner promised that his administration would be bipartisan, consisting of both Democrats and Republicans. "Mindful of those who have preceded me and humbled by the oath that I have taken," Warner stated in his inaugural speech, "I make this solemn pledge: to honor your trust, to earn your respect, and to work to ensure that this Commonwealth assumes her rightful place as a leader among the states of our great nation."[2]

Both Thomas Jefferson (left) and James Monroe (right) served as governors of Virginia before becoming presidents of the United States.

▶ The Judicial Branch

The state's Supreme Court is one of the oldest judicial bodies in the United States. In 1779 the General Assembly created four superior courts, including the Supreme Court of Appeals. The Supreme Court of Appeals was a model for the Supreme Court of the United States. Edmund Pendleton, who was a delegate to the First Continental Congress, served as the first president of the Supreme Court of Appeals, a role that we would now call chief justice. In 1970 the state constitution changed the name of the court to the Supreme Court of Virginia.

The present Supreme Court of Virginia consists of seven justices, who are elected to twelve-year terms by a majority vote of both houses of the General Assembly. The justice who has served on the court for the longest time is appointed the chief justice. The Supreme Court of Virginia is the highest court in a statewide judicial system that includes the Virginia Court of Appeals, circuit courts, general district courts, and juvenile and domestic-relations courts. The high court's primary role is to review the decisions of lower courts.

Chapter 5 ▶

Liberty or Death: History

The mountains and shorelines of Virginia were populated long before English colonists settled there. The earliest known residents of the Virginia region were Indian tribes of three major language groups, including the Powhatan tribe. In addition to growing corn, these tribes also grew tobacco, which would eventually become Virginia's most important crop. In the late 1500s, the Powhatan tribe may have had as many as 15,000 members.

In 1584, Queen Elizabeth I of England sent Sir Walter Raleigh to establish colonies in the New World. Although the colonists landed along the coast of what is now North Carolina, Raleigh named the region "Virginia." Raleigh's colonists on Roanoke Island did not survive, and little is known about their fate. By 1607, however, the first permanent English settlement was built at Jamestown.

▶ Colonial Virginia

At first, life was difficult in the settlement, which was infested with disease-carrying mosquitoes and occasionally attacked by American Indians. Many of the colonists, believing themselves to be gentlemen who should not do hard work, often refused to perform manual labor and plant crops. It was left to Captain John Smith to become a leader of the struggling colony. He established a rule that "he that will not worke, shall not eate."[1] By 1609, however, the colonists were nearly starving, and many had died. The settlement might have collapsed were it not

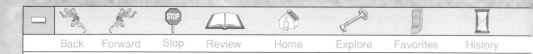
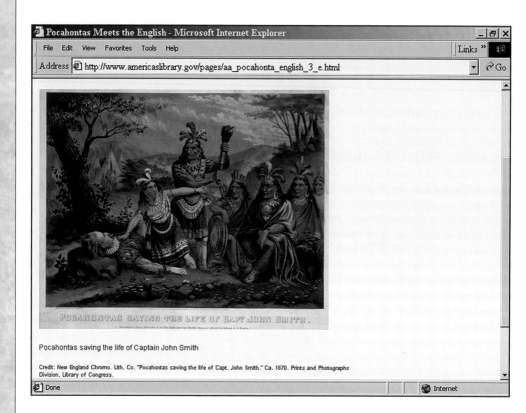

Pocahontas saving the life of Captain John Smith

Credit: New England Chromo. Lith. Co. "Pocahontas saving the life of Capt. John Smith." Ca. 1870. Prints and Photographs Division, Library of Congress.

▲ The daughter of Chief Powhatan, Pocahontas is seen intervening to save the life of Captain John Smith in this nineteenth-century painting.

for John Rolfe, a settler who planted a popular kind of tobacco, and other colonists who worked to establish a profitable industry. In 1614, Rolfe married Pocahontas, daughter of Chief Powhatan, and their marriage helped to keep the peace between the colonists and the native tribes.

But peace did not last long. By the mid-1600s, colonists began to tire of English rule. Nathaniel Bacon, a planter from Henrico County, had several arguments with local Indians that led to violence. The British governor of Virginia forbade him from attacking the tribes, but Bacon and a group of colonists defied the government and attacked anyway.

By the 1700s, Virginia's capital had moved from Jamestown to Williamsburg, and disputes with local tribes continued. The French and Indian War, from 1754 to 1763, engaged British, French, and American Indian forces in a fight for territory. The British won, which meant that the Virginia colony could continue to expand.

▶ Stirrings Toward Independence

By the late 1770s, Virginians, like other colonists, had become frustrated with the British government's taxation policies. Colonists began organizing their own meetings to shape colonial policies. In August 1774, the First Virginia Convention met in Williamsburg and arranged to send delegates to the First Continental Congress in Philadelphia in September. There, a Virginian named Peyton Randolph was chosen president of the congress. But it was at the Second Virginia Convention, held in Richmond the following March, that Virginians were most strongly urged to fight for independence. Patrick Henry, a patriot from Hanover County, Virginia, argued that, by tightening its grip on the colonies, the British government had already started a war. "The war is inevitable—and let it come!" Henry exclaimed. He ended with his famous cry "I know not what course others may take, but as for me, give me liberty or give me death!"[2]

▶ The Revolutionary War

In April 1775 a colonial militia engaged in the first battles of the Revolutionary War at Lexington and Concord in Massachusetts. The following month, Virginian George Washington became the Continental Army's commander

Welcome to Gunston Hall Plantation - Microsoft Internet Explorer

File   Edit   View   Favorites   Tools   Help   Links »

Address http://gunstonhall.org/welcome   Go

Gunston Hall Plantation

Welcome to Gunston Hall

"That all men are born equally free and independent, and have certain inherent natural Rights . . . among which are the Enjoyment of Life and Liberty, with the Means of acquiring and possessing Property, and pursueing and obtaining Happiness and Safety."

-- George Mason
First Draft of the Virginia Declaration of Rights, written in May, 1776. Published in final form at Williamsburg on June 12, 1776

Photo by Dennis McWaters

Done   Internet

The writings of colonial statesman and Virginian George Mason inspired the thinking of the founding fathers, especially fellow Virginian Thomas Jefferson. Mason's home, Gunston Hall Plantation, is a National Historic Landmark.

in chief. Small battles took place around the Norfolk and Hampton Roads areas later that fall, and by the following year, the war for independence was well underway. On July 4, 1776, the Continental Congress adopted the Declaration of Independence, written by Thomas Jefferson. Two days later, Patrick Henry began his term as Virginia's first state governor.

It was after a battle at Yorktown, Virginia, on October 1781, that the British army finally surrendered. By that time, Virginia's capital had moved from Williamsburg to its permanent location in Richmond.

Early Virginia Leaders

As the new United States prepared for self-government, Virginia once again took the lead. The first Virginia constitution included a declaration of rights written by Virginian George Mason, which became the basis for the Bill of Rights in the U.S. Constitution. Four of the nation's first five presidents were from Virginia—George Washington, Thomas Jefferson, James Madison, and James Monroe. These men were sometimes called the Virginia

▲ It was at Yorktown, Virginia, in October 1781 that the British army surrendered to American and French forces, bringing an end to the fighting in the Revolutionary War. A reenactment of the Battle of Yorktown is pictured.

Dynasty and were greatly admired. Before Washington retired to Mount Vernon, he composed his Farewell Address. "I anticipate with pleasing expectation that retreat," Washington wrote, "in which I promise myself to realize . . . the sweet enjoyment of partaking, in the midst of my fellow Citizens, the benign influence of good Laws under a free Government. . . ."[3]

The Nineteenth Century

Over the next few decades, Virginians continued to defend and guide the young nation. During the War of 1812, the

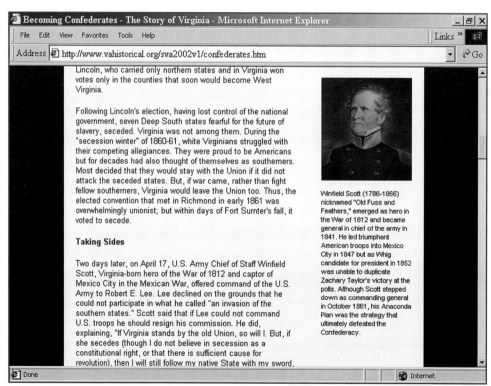

Becoming Confederates - The Story of Virginia - Microsoft Internet Explorer

File Edit View Favorites Tools Help   Links »

Address http://www.vahistorical.org/sva2002v1/confederates.htm   Go

Lincoln, who carried only northern states and in Virginia won votes only in the counties that soon would become West Virginia.

Following Lincoln's election, having lost control of the national government, seven Deep South states fearful for the future of slavery, seceded. Virginia was not among them. During the "secession winter" of 1860-61, white Virginians struggled with their competing allegiances. They were proud to be Americans but for decades had also thought of themselves as southerners. Most decided that they would stay with the Union if it did not attack the seceded states. But, if war came, rather than fight fellow southerners, Virginia would leave the Union too. Thus, the elected convention that met in Richmond in early 1861 was overwhelmingly unionist; but within days of Fort Sumter's fall, it voted to secede.

Taking Sides

Two days later, on April 17, U.S. Army Chief of Staff Winfield Scott, Virginia-born hero of the War of 1812 and captor of Mexico City in the Mexican War, offered command of the U.S. Army to Robert E. Lee. Lee declined on the grounds that he could not participate in what he called "an invasion of the southern states." Scott said that if Lee could not command U.S. troops he should resign his commission. He did, explaining, "If Virginia stands by the old Union, so will I. But, if she secedes (though I do not believe in secession as a constitutional right, or that there is sufficient cause for revolution), then I will still follow my native State with my sword.

Winfield Scott (1786-1866) nicknamed "Old Fuss and Feathers," emerged as hero in the War of 1812 and became general in chief of the army in 1841. He led triumphant American troops into Mexico City in 1847 but as Whig candidate for president in 1852 was unable to duplicate Zachary Taylor's victory at the polls. Although Scott stepped down as commanding general in October 1861, his Anaconda Plan was the strategy that ultimately defeated the Confederacy.

Done   Internet

General Winfield Scott had been the general-in-chief of the U.S. Army for two decades by the time the Civil War began. A Petersburg, Virginia, native, Scott refused to join the Confederacy. He was the Union army's commanding general at the start of the war.

Tools   Search   Notes   Discuss   Go!

British navy raided towns along the Virginia coastline, burning Washington, D.C., in 1814. William Henry Harrison and Winfield Scott were among the Virginians who successfully held back British forces at several points during the war. Harrison became president, although he served for only one month of his term before dying. John Tyler, his vice president and a Virginian, succeeded him. Along with Virginian Zachary Taylor (another future president), Scott led the U.S. Army to victory five years later in the Mexican-American War.

Between North and South

A result of the Mexican-American War was that the boundaries of the United States expanded to include Texas, New Mexico, Arizona, and much of California. But the addition of new territory to the nation increased the debate over whether the practice of slavery should be expanded westward. Already, people in the North were calling for the abolition, or ending, of slavery. But people in the South wanted to continue slavery, which they felt was necessary to their way of life.

Nat Turner's Rebellion

Slavery had been allowed in Virginia since the earliest settlement at Jamestown. In 1831, Nat Turner, a leader among many slaves, led a bloody slave rebellion in Southampton County, Virginia, in which more than fifty white people were killed. The revolt was put down quickly, and thirteen slaves and three free black people were hanged for what has come to be known as the Southampton Insurrection. Turner, who had escaped but was captured after six weeks in hiding, was also hanged. The revolt led to even more oppressive laws for slaves

in the South, and tensions between North and South continued to rise.

▶ Secession

Late in 1860 and early in 1861, South Carolina and ten other southern states chose to secede, or withdraw, from the Union. Virginia seceded in April 1861. The southern states called themselves the Confederate States of America. Montgomery, Alabama, was their capital for the first four months, and then Richmond, Virginia, became the capital of the Confederacy. Robert E. Lee, a loyal soldier in the U.S. Army, who had fought in Mexico, made the difficult decision to join the Confederacy. "My husband has wept tears of blood over this terrible war," Lee's wife, Mary Custis Lee, once wrote, "but as a man of honor and a Virginian, he must follow the destiny of his state."[4] Lee became the Confederacy's most famous general.

◀ Robert E. Lee, a member of one of Virginia's most influential families, has been hailed as one of the greatest military figures of the Civil War.

Tools   Search   Notes   Discuss   Go!

▶ Civil War Battles Fought on Virginia Soil

Because it was so close to Washington, D.C., and because its farmland and other industries were so important to the Confederacy, Virginia was crucial to the defense of both the Union and the Confederacy. More major Civil War battles were fought in Virginia than in any other state. The first major battle took place in July 1861 near Manassas, Virginia, along a stream called Bull Run. (The North generally named battles after waterways or landmarks. The South named battles after the closest city or town. Thus the battle is called both Bull Run and Manassas.) It was a one-sided victory for the Confederates, who followed this victory with another one on the same ground in August 1862.

At the first battle of Manassas, Thomas J. Jackson, a soldier and professor from Clarksburg, Virginia, earned his legendary nickname "Stonewall." Some accounts of the battle say that he earned the nickname when General Barnard Bee, urging his men to be brave, said, "There is Jackson standing like a stone wall! Rally behind the Virginians!"[5] Jackson led his regiments, known as the Stonewall Brigade, to several Confederate victories in the Shenandoah Valley in 1862. That December, the Union also suffered a crushing defeat at Fredericksburg, Virginia.

The tide of war began to favor the Union army in Virginia and the rest of the South in 1863. That May, in Chancellorsville, not far from Fredericksburg, Confederate soldiers accidentally shot Stonewall Jackson, who died a few days later. In June, Virginia's northwestern counties, which had voted to stay with the Union, officially became the separate state of West Virginia. By July, Lee's army suffered major losses at Gettysburg, Pennsylvania. Although the war continued for two more bloody years,

the Confederacy was never able to regain its footing. On April 9, 1865, Lee surrendered to General Ulysses S. Grant at Appomattox Court House, Virginia.

With the end of the Civil War came the end of the institution of slavery and the strengthening of the United States. In 1869, Virginia adopted a new constitution that gave African Americans the right to vote. Virginia was readmitted to the Union in 1870.

▶ The Early Twentieth Century

At the turn of the twentieth century, Virginia's industries were booming, especially in cigarette manufacturing, cotton textiles, and shipbuilding. But even as the state became more modernized, policies and laws seemed to be moving backward toward the Civil War. In the late 1800s, the state government began to systematically pass laws that prevented freed slaves from voting or being elected to public office. The state constitution of 1902 officially enacted a segregated, or separated, school system, meaning that white children and black children could not attend the same schools.

Although race relations were strained, the state was preoccupied with war during the first half of the twentieth century. In 1912, Woodrow Wilson, who was born in Staunton and later studied at the University of Virginia, was elected president of the United States. Wilson tried to keep the country out of World War I, but eventually agreed that the nation would have to fight.

In the late 1920s, Harry F. Byrd had become a political powerhouse in Virginia. As governor, Byrd helped to streamline state government. In 1933, he began a thirty-year career in the U.S. Senate. A Democrat, Byrd was determined to lower taxes and reduce the size and spending of the federal government, positions often associated with the Republican Party.

World War II and After

With America's entrance into World War II, in 1941, the population in northern Virginia began to soar, as people came to the nation's capital to work in the federal government. Civilians also filled jobs in the shipyards and military bases in Newport News and along the lower James River. In 1943, construction was completed on the Pentagon, the massive five-sided headquarters of the Department of Defense, in Arlington.

Despite the economic and industrial boom of the postwar years, the divide between the races was wider than ever. In 1956, to oppose the federal desegregation of schools, the Virginia legislature passed a law that allowed the state to close any school that had been desegregated. But federal and state courts later overturned this law. By 1959, public schools had started to integrate, and the state was completely integrated by the late 1960s. In 1967, William Reid became the first African American elected to the Virginia state legislature since 1891.

And in one of the most symbolic efforts to close the racial divide, in 1996 a statue of Arthur Ashe, a famous African-American tennis player, was dedicated on a Richmond avenue lined with Confederate monuments.

Modern Virginia

According to the 2000 United States census, Virginia is the twelfth most populous state, with 7,078,515 residents. Nearly 20 percent of the population is African American, and just over half of Virginia residents are female.

▲ *On June 11, 2002, Deputy Secretary of Defense Paul Wolfowitz spoke at a ceremony in which a time capsule was dedicated, to be inserted into the rebuilt western façade of the Pentagon, in Arlington, Virginia. The salvaged engraved limestone bearing the date of the terrorist attacks was one of the building's original stones.*

On September 11, 2001, the deadliest terrorist attacks in U.S. history took place in New York and Virginia. Hijackers crashed planes into the World Trade Center in New York City, and the Pentagon, in Arlington. Nearly 200 people died in the Pentagon attack. But construction crews worked quickly to rebuild the outer ring of the historic building by the one-year anniversary of the attacks. Many of the workers were immigrants to the United States who had settled in Virginia. "I've never seen a job where everybody's this committed," a foreman said of the reconstruction.[6]

The dedication of the crews who rebuilt the Pentagon is an accurate reflection of Virginians over the past four centuries. If the past is a guide, Virginia will continue to be a leader in industry and technology for centuries to come.

Chapter Notes

Chapter 1. Virginia: Witness to History

1. B. L. Rayner, *Life of Thomas Jefferson* (Boston: Lilly, Wait, Colman, & Holden, 1834), chapter 38, electronic text, The University of Virginia Library, n.d., <http://etext.lib .virginia.edu/jefferson/biog/lj38.htm> (June 26, 2002).

Chapter 2. Mountains to the Sea: Land and Climate

1. Matthew Page Andrews, *Virginia: The Old Dominion, Volume I* (Richmond, Va.: The Dietz Press, 1949), p. 19.

Chapter 3. Tobacco to Technology: Economy

1. Matthew Page Andrews, *Virginia: The Old Dominion, Volume I* (Richmond, Va.: The Dietz Press, 1949), p. 10.

2. Dan Upson, Virginia Secretary of Technology, *Virginia Economic Development Partnership,* Office of the Governor press release, "Governor Gilmore Announces America Online's Selection of Prince William County. . ." March 10, 1999, <www.yesvirginia.org/newsitem.asp?ID= 126>.

Chapter 4. For the Good of the Commonwealth: Government

1. Alf J. Mapp, Jr., *The Virginia Experiment: The Old Dominion's Role in the Making of America (1607–1781)* (Richmond, Va.: The Dietz Press, 1957), p. 47.

2. *The Official Website of the Governor of Virginia,* "The Inaugural Remarks of the Honorable Mark R. Warner," January 12, 2002, <www.governor.state.va.us/Press_Policy/ Major_Events/Inauguration/Inauguration_Speech.html>.

Chapter 5. Liberty or Death: History

1. Emily J. Salmon and Edward D. C. Campbell, Jr., eds., *The Hornbook of Virginia History* (Richmond, Va.: The Library of Virginia, 1994), p. 10.

2. Stephen Ambrose and Douglas Brinkley, *Witness to America: An Illustrated Documentary History of the United States from the Revolution to Today* (New York: HarperCollins, 1999), p. 9.

3. The University of Virginia, *The Papers of George Washington*, "Washington's Farewell Address," <www.virginia.edu/gwpapers/farewell/transcript.html> (May 5, 2002).

4. Douglas Southall Freeman (abridgement by Richard Harwell), *Lee* (New York: Collier Books, MacMillan Publishing Company, 1991), p. 112.

5. James M. McPherson, *Battle Cry of Freedom: The Civil War Era* (New York and Oxford: Oxford University Press, 1988), p. 342.

6. Andrea Stone, "Pentagon Crew Imposes Tight Deadline on Itself," *USA Today*, March 10, 2002, <http://usatoday.com/news/attack/2002/03/11/usat-pentagon.htm>.

Further Reading

Ambrose, Stephen, and Douglas Brinkley. *Witness to America: An Illustrated Documentary History of the United States from the Revolution to Today.* New York: HarperCollins, 1999.

Barrett, Tracy. *Celebrate the States: Virginia.* Tarrytown, N.Y.: Benchmark Books, 1997.

Beller, Susan Provost. *The Confederate Ladies of Richmond.* Brookfield, Conn.: Twenty-first Century Books, 1999.

Coleman, Brooke. *The Colony of Virginia.* New York: Rosen Publishing Group, 1999.

DeAngelis, Gina. *Virginia.* Danbury, Conn.: Children's Press, 2001.

Fradin, Dennis Brindell. *The Virginia Colony.* Chicago: Children's Press, 1986.

Goor, Ron, and Nancy Goor. *Williamsburg: Cradle of the Revolution.* New York: Atheneum Books for Young Readers, 1994.

Pollack, Pamela. *Virginia: The Old Dominion.* Milwaukee: Gareth Stevens, 2002.

Index